Table of Contents

Angel Hair Pasta with Savory Mushroom Sauce

Artichoke and Angel Hair Pasta

Avocado Pasta

Basil Garlic Linguine

Creamy Macaroni & "Cheese"

Creamy Red Pepper Lentil Lasagna

Creamy Spinach Pesto

Delicious Vegan Lasagna

Easy Artichoke Pesto Pasta

Easy Cheesy Lasagna

Eggplant, Tomato, and Garlic Pasta

Eggplant Penne

Fettuccini with Chanterelle and Olive Sauce

Lentil Spaghetti

Linguine with Tomatoes

Mushroom Spinach Ravioli with Pesto Cream

Penne Primavera with Alfredo Sauce

Roasted Beet Ravioli with Sage Pesto Sauce

Roasted Red Pepper Pesto

Seared Shitakes, Walnut, and Spinach Linguine in a Butter Cream Sauce

Southwestern Linguine Toss

Soy Sausage and Broccoli Baked Ziti

Spinach and Mushroom Fettuccine Alfredo

Tofu Florentine with Angel Hair Pasta

Tofu Manicotti

Tomato, Basil, and Roasted Pine Nut Penne

Tomato and Basil Spaghetti

Vegetable Linguine

Angel Hair Pasta with Savory Mushroom Sauce

Preparation Time: 15 minutes
Cooking Time: 25 minutes
Serves: 4

Ingredients

1-(16 ounce) package angel hair pasta
2 (8 ounce) trays white mushrooms
1/4 cup extra virgin olive oil
6 cloves garlic, peeled
1/2 cup fresh basil leaves
1/2 cup fresh parsley
Juice of 1 lemon
2 tablespoons soy sauce
Salt and white pepper, to taste
1 pound Portobello mushrooms, broken in pieces

Directions

1. Prepare pasta by cooking it in salted water until al dente, according to package directions. Drain and set aside.
2. Slice 4 ounces of the white mushrooms, and set aside.
3. In a food processor, add garlic and olive oil, and pulse until the garlic is minced. Add the unsliced white mushrooms, basil, parsley, lemon juice, soy sauce, dash salt and several dashes white pepper; pulse until the vegetables are well minced.
4. Add Portobello mushrooms to the food processor; pulse until Portobello mushrooms are very coarsely chopped.
5. In a sauté pan or skillet over high heat, add the mushrooms mixture and the chopped mushrooms, stirring constantly until the mixture comes to a boil.
6. Reduce heat to medium-high until the liquid is reduced by about one-half; it should be a similar consistency to marinara sauce.
7. Place pasta on serving dishes, and top with sauce.

Artichoke and Angel Hair Pasta

Preparation Time: 5 minutes
Cooking Time: 40 minutes
Serves: 2 to 4

Ingredients

1-(8 ounce) box angel hair pasta
1-(15 ounce) can diced organic fire roasted tomatoes
1-(6 ounce) jar capers
2-(8 ounce) jars marinated artichoke hearts
1-(2.25 ounce) can chopped black olives
3 cloves garlic
1 to 2 tablespoons olive oil
1 bay leaf
1 tablespoon oregano

Directions

1. In a skillet, heat olive oil over high heat for 2 minutes. Add garlic and sauté for another 2 minutes. Add tomatoes, bay leaf, and oregano and let cook for 5 minutes. Stirring occasionally.
2. Reduce heat to simmer and add capers, artichoke hearts, and black olives. Simmer for about 15 minutes. Add Salt and pepper, to taste
3. While sauce is simmering, prepare angel hair pasta according to the directions on the box. Drain pasta.
4. Place pasta on serving dishes, and top with sauce.

Avocado Pasta

Preparation Time: 10 minutes
Cooking Time: 20 minutes
Serves: 2

Ingredients

1/2 of a 16-ounce package whole grain pasta (of choice), cooked and drained
1 cup sprouts or a leafy green
2 tablespoons olive oil
2 tablespoon fresh chives or green onion, chopped
2 tablespoon fresh mint, chopped
1 tablespoon nutritional yeast
2 cloves garlic, pressed
1 lime, zested and juiced
Pinch salt
Pinch pepper
1 avocado, sliced

Directions

1. Cook pasta according to package directions. Drain, and then return it to the pot.
2. Stir in the sprouts, olive oil, chives, mint, nutritional yeast, garlic, lime zest, lime juice, salt, and pepper.
3. Serve the pasta topped with sliced avocado and freshly ground pepper.

Basil Garlic Linguine

Preparation Time: 10 minutes
Cooking Time: 15 minutes
Serves: 4

Ingredients

8 ounces whole grain linguine
Sauce:
1 tablespoon balsamic vinegar
1 tablespoon olive oil
1-(15-ounce) can crushed tomatoes, lightly drained
4 to 5 medium cloves garlic, pressed or minced
2 teaspoons dried oregano
1/4 cup fresh basil, cut into thin ribbons
1 teaspoon sea salt
Black pepper, to taste

Directions

1. Begin cooking the linguine according to the directions on the package.
2. While the noodles are cooking, add sauce ingredients to a large bowl and mix them together.
3. When linguine is al dente, drain and toss it with the sauce.
4. Serve immediately.

Creamy Macaroni & "Cheese"

Preparation Time: 30 minutes
Cooking Time: 30 minutes
Serves: 10
Ingredients
Macaroni and Cheese:
16 ounces elbow macaroni
3 tablespoons vegan margarine
1 cup white onion, chopped
3 medium cloves garlic, minced
8 ounces vegan cream cheese, softened
2-1/2 cups unsweetened nondairy milk
2 tablespoons nutritional yeast
1-1/2 teaspoons salt
1/2 teaspoon paprika
Pinch cayenne pepper
Pinch black pepper
3 cups shredded vegan cheddar cheese

Topping
1/4 cup vegan buttery spread
1 cup panko (Japanese-style breadcrumbs)
1 teaspoon dried dill
3/4 teaspoon dried thyme

Directions
1. Prepare pasta according to package directions. Set aside.
2. Preheat oven to 350 degrees F. Lightly grease a 9x13-inch glass baking dish.
3. In a large pot, over medium heat, melt 3 tablespoons of vegan margarine. Add onion and garlic and cook, stirring frequently, for 3 to 5 minutes, or until onion is translucent.
4. Reduce heat to low and add cream cheese, milk, nutritional yeast, salt, paprika, cayenne pepper, black pepper, and cheddar cheese, stirring frequently until mixture is thoroughly combined, and cheeses are melted.
5. Remove from heat and add cooked pasta, stirring until pasta is evenly coated. Pour into the prepared baking dish and set aside.
6. Topping: melt 1/4 cup vegan margarine over medium heat. Add panko, dill and thyme, stirring until combined, about 1 minute. Turn off

heat and pour topping evenly over pasta mixture.
7.   Place baking pan in the oven, and bake for 20 to 30 minutes, or until mixture is bubbly and topping is light golden brown.

Creamy Red Pepper Lentil Lasagna

Preparation Time: 35 minutes
Cooking Time: 1 hour
Serves: 4
Ingredients
12 lasagna noodles
2-(15 ounce) cans red lentils, drained
2 red bell peppers, chopped
1 onion, chopped
Olive oil, as needed
4 cups tomato pasta sauce (of choice)
1 teaspoon oregano
1 teaspoon basil
1 teaspoon thyme
Salt and pepper, to taste
3 tablespoons vegan butter
2 to 3 tablespoons flour
2 cups nondairy milk

Directions
1. Preheat oven to 325 degrees F.
2. Cook lasagna noodles according to package directions.
3. Boil lentils with water in a medium sized pot for 30 minutes.
4. In a skillet, add olive oil, cook the onion and red pepper over medium-high heat until onion becomes translucent; around 6 to 8 minutes.
5. Drain and rinse the lentils when they are cooked, and then add them to the pan with the vegetables.
6. Add the tomato sauce and spices, and cook the mixture for a few minutes.
7. Coat the bottom of a 9x13-inch lasagna baking pan with a thin layer of tomato sauce.
8. Place a layer of lasagna noodles in the baking pan; then a layer of the lentil mixture; then a layer of noodles; then a layer of the lentil mixture; and finally another layer of noodles.
9. Topping: In a small sauce pan, melt vegan butter. When it is melted, remove from heat and add flour, and mix well. Add flour as needed until becomes thick and creamy. Add 1 cup of nondairy milk, stir

well, and heat on medium-high heat. Stir constantly.

10. When the sauce starts to thicken, add a second cup of milk. Keep stirring until the sauce begins to thicken, then reduce heat and let sit for 2 to 3 minutes, stirring occasionally. When the sauce is thick, like Alfredo sauce, pour it over the top of the lasagna.

11. Place baking pan in the oven, and bake for about 1 hour.

Creamy Spinach Pesto

Preparation Time: 10 minutes
Cooking Time: 5 minutes
Serves: 2
Ingredients

1 pound pasta
2 cups fresh spinach, packed
1/2 cup nondairy milk (I use soy)
2 cloves garlic
1/4 cup almonds
2 tablespoons olive oil
2 tablespoons vegan margarine
1 teaspoon sea salt
1/4 teaspoon cayenne pepper
1/2 teaspoon ground black pepper

Directions

1. Cook pasta according to package directions.
2. Place all of the other ingredients in a blender, and blend until smooth.
3. Transfer blended ingredients to a saucepan, and cook over medium heat for about 5 minutes, until bubbly and slightly thickened.
4. Drain pasta, and stir in pesto.
5. Serve.

Delicious Vegan Lasagna

Preparation Time: 45 minutes
Cooking Time: 50 minutes
Serves: 8

Ingredients

1-(24 ounce) jar spaghetti sauce (of choice)
1 tablespoon olive oil, for sautéing
4 ounces canned mushrooms
1 medium onion, chopped
2 links vegan sausage, sliced
4 ounces black olives, sliced
4 ounces green olives, sliced
14 ounces extra-firm tofu, squeezed
3 cloves garlic, minced
1/8 teaspoon pepper
1/4 teaspoon salt
2 teaspoons olive oil
1/2 cup nutritional yeast
16 ounces precooked lasagna noodles

Directions

1. Cook lasagna noodles according to package directions.
2. Preheat your oven to 375 degrees F.
3. In a small pot, heat sauce according to the directions on the jar, or on medium-high. When sauce becomes warm, reduce heat to low.
4. In a frying pan, heat 1 tablespoon of olive oil over medium-high heat, and sauté the mushrooms, onion, and sausage until the onion is transparent and the sausage is slightly browned. When the mushrooms, onion, and sausage are cooked, add them to sauce.
5. Add green and black olives to the sauce. Continue to simmer sauce over low heat.
6. In a large mixing bowl, crumble tofu to a ricotta cheese texture. Add garlic, salt, pepper, 2 teaspoons olive oil, and nutritional yeast to the tofu, and mix well with a fork until the tofu is coated with nutritional yeast.
7. Coat the bottom of a 7x9-inch lasagna baking pan with a thin layer of the sauce.
8. Add 2 layers of 2 lasagna noodles; Then, add a layer of sauce.

9. Layer the tofu cheese on top of the noodles. Spread it evenly with a fork..
10. Add two layers of lasagna noodles, one layer of sauce, one layer of cheese, and so on, until all of the ingredients are used. Set aside some sauce to top the lasagna.
11. Cover with two layers of aluminum foil, and bake for 30 minutes. Then remove the layers of foil and bake uncovered for an additional 20 minutes.
12. Remove lasagna from oven and let it cool for 10 minutes.
13. Slice and serve.

Easy Artichoke Pesto Pasta

Preparation Time: 15 minutes
Cooking Time: 15 minutes
Serves: 6

Ingredients

1 pound ziti pasta
1/3 cup pecans, chopped
3 cloves garlic, minced
1/2 lemon, juiced
1-(14 ounce) can artichoke hearts in water, drained and chopped
8 fresh basil leaves, chopped
2 tablespoons fresh parsley, chopped
2 tablespoons nutritional yeast
1/4 cup olive oil
1/4 to 1/3 cup reserved pasta water
Salt and ground black pepper, to taste

Directions

1. Cook pasta according to package directions. Add some salt and olive oil.
2. Meanwhile, add pecans and garlic to a food processor, and pulse until finely chopped.
3. Add the remaining ingredients to the food processor, and blend until it becomes a smooth sauce. Taste and adjust salt and pepper as needed.
4. Reserve some pasta water before draining pasta. Drain pasta and put it back into the cooking pot.
5. Pour the sauce over the pasta. Stir together, adding pasta water as needed to thin the sauce to cover the pasta, while maintaining a creamy sauce consistency.
6. Serve immediately.

Easy Cheesy Lasagna

Preparation Time: 15 minutes
Cooking Time: 1 hour
Serves: 6

Ingredients

1-(10 ounce) package vegan mozzarella cheese, shredded
1-(10 ounce) package vegan cheddar cheese, shredded
1-(32 ounce) jar pasta sauce, divided
1-(8 ounce) can tomato sauce
12 lasagna noodles, uncooked
2-(3-1/2 ounce) vegan Italian sausages, thinly sliced

Directions

1. Preheat oven to 450 degrees F. In a bowl, combine the shredded mozzarella and cheddar cheeses together.
2. In a separate bowl, combine the pasta and tomato sauces. Spread a thin layer of sauce along the bottom of a 9x13-inch baking dish.
3. Cover the bottom of dish with 1 layer of lasagna noodles and spread a thin layer of pasta sauce over the noodles. Distribute half of the sliced sausage over the sauce. Spread 1/3 the cheese mixture evenly over the noodles, sauce, and sausage.
4. Repeat previous step.
5. Finish with a layer of lasagna noodles and the remaining pasta sauce, ensuring that all noodles are covered in sauce. Top with remaining 1/3 cheese mixture.
6. Cover and bake for 45 to 50 minutes. Remove cover and broil for about 5 minutes, until cheese is lightly browned and bubbling.

Eggplant, Tomato, and Garlic Pasta

Preparation Time: 10 minutes
Cooking Time: 30 minutes
Serves: 4

Ingredients

1 medium eggplant
6 ounces artichoke hearts
1-(16 ounce) can diced tomatoes (do not drain)
1/2 cup vegetable broth
3 cloves garlic, crushed
Dried basil and oregano, to taste
1 (8 ounce) package angel hair pasta
Olive oil for cooking
Dash of crushed red pepper flakes

Directions

1. Cook pasta according to package directions.
2. Peel eggplant and cut into 1/2-inch cubes.
3. In a small pot, heat olive oil over medium heat, sauté eggplant cubes, turning frequently to prevent burning. Add artichoke hearts. Cook until eggplant begins to soften.
4. Add the can of tomatoes, un-drained, and the vegetable broth. Add crushed garlic, basil, oregano, and crushed red pepper flakes, to taste.
5. Stir entire mixture and simmer for about 10 to 15 minutes.
6. Serve over pasta.

Eggplant Penne

Preparation Time: 15 minutes
Cooking Time: 30 minutes
Serves: 6

Ingredients

1 pound whole wheat penne pasta
1 red onion, sliced into rings
5 Eggplants
6 cloves garlic, minced
1 large tomato, diced
1/4 cup sundried tomatoes
1/2 cup whole, pitted Kalamata olives
Extra virgin olive oil
1/4 cup dry red wine
1 teaspoon oregano
1 teaspoon basil
Salt, to taste

Directions

1. Cook pasta according to package directions. When the pasta is cooked, toss is a small amount of extra virgin olive oil.
2. Meanwhile, in a large skillet, sauté the onions in oil over medium-high heat until they brown. Cook until caramelized, and then transfer them to a bowl. Set aside.
3. In the same pan, add a little bit more oil and sauté garlic for about 15 seconds. Add diced eggplant, and sprinkle with salt. Cook until the eggplant becomes very soft, stirring often so that it cooks evenly. Add the diced tomatoes and olives. Cook for 2 minutes. Add wine, oregano, and basil. Cook for an additional 5 minutes.
4. Remove from heat and stir in the sundried tomatoes and caramelized onions.
5. Serve over prepared pasta.

Fettuccini with Chanterelle and Olive Sauce

Preparation Time: 10 minutes
Cooking Time: 10 minutes
Serves: 2
Ingredients
5 ounces uncooked fettuccini pasta
5 ounces chanterelle mushrooms
10 black olives, chopped
1 garlic clove, chopped
1 tablespoon margarine
1/4 cup soymilk
Parsley, to taste
Salt and pepper, to taste
Parsley, to garnish
Directions
1. Bring water to boil and begin cooking your pasta according to package directions.
2. Meanwhile, wash and tear mushrooms in small pieces.
3. In a skillet heat vegan margarine and add garlic. Cook for about 30 seconds, and then add mushrooms and spices and fry them until they start to release their juices. If the liquid evaporates, the mushrooms will be rubbery. So fry them for approximately 3 minutes, and then add soy milk and chopped olives.
4. Drain pasta, and add it to the sauce.
5. Heat together for about 1 minute.
6. Serve and garnish with chopped parsley.

Lentil Spaghetti

Preparation Time: 10 minutes
Cooking Time: 45 minutes
Serves: 5 to 6

Ingredients

4 cups water
Dash salt
1 cup brown or French green lentils
Olive oil
1 onion, sliced
4 cloves garlic, minced
1-(24 ounce) jar spaghetti sauce (of choice)
1-(15-ounce) can diced tomatoes, drained
Herbs, to taste (basil, marjoram, oregano, thyme, and chives.)
2-(8-ounce) packages whole wheat pasta, cooked and drained
Black pepper, to taste
Pinch sugar, or to taste
Small pinch turmeric

Directions

1. Cook pasta according to package instructions.
2. Fill a small pot with water. Add a dash of salt, and lentils. Bring to boil over medium-high heat, uncovered, stirring every few minutes, until lentils are tender.
3. Meanwhile, heat olive oil in a skillet over medium-high heat. Add onions and cook until slightly softened. Add garlic and sauté for two minutes. Add tomato sauce and tomatoes. Reduce heat to medium. Add a splash more oil.
4. When lentils are tender, drain them and add them to the sauce.
5. Add herbs, black pepper, sugar, and turmeric.
6. Serve over cooked pasta.

Linguine with Tomatoes

Preparation Time: 10 minutes
Cooking Time: 30 minutes
Serves: 6

Ingredients

1 pound box linguine
4 to 6 large tomatoes, diced
1-(6 ounce) jar sliced green olives
1-(4 ounce) can sliced black olives
1/4 cup olive oil
1/2 tablespoon Basil
1 cup vegan mozzarella cheese, shredded
Salt and pepper, to taste

Directions

1. Cook linguine according to package directions. Drain, and drizzle with a little of the olive oil to prevent it from sticking together. Let cool.
2. Dice tomatoes and place them in a large bowl. Add olives, basil, salt, pepper, and olive oil. Allow this mixture to marinate for at least 20 minutes.
3. Add pasta to tomato mixture.
4. Add vegan cheese, and serve.

Mushroom Spinach Ravioli with Pesto Cream

Preparation Time: 25 minutes
Cooking Time: 30 minutes
Serves: 4

Ingredients

1/2 medium onion, minced
2 cloves minced garlic
2 Portabella mushrooms, roughly chopped
10 shiitake mushrooms, roughly chopped
1 bag baby spinach
1 package (15 ounce block) regular firm tofu
1-1/2 teaspoon dried basil
1-1/2 teaspoon dried oregano
1/2 cup finely shredded vegan mozzarella
1 package vegan wonton wraps
1 cup plain soymilk

Pesto:

1/2 cup sun-dried tomatoes
3/4 cup packed fresh basil
2 cloves chopped garlic
1/4 cup toasted pine nuts
1 teaspoon crushed red pepper flakes
1/4 cup shredded parmesan vegan cheese

Directions

1. Add all pesto ingredients to a food processor. Add salt and pepper to taste. Blend, adding extra virgin olive oil, until it just barely comes together into a paste. Remove pesto from the food processor, place it in a bowl, and set it aside.
2. Rinse food processor. Add mushrooms and pulse chop into small pieces.
3. Over medium heat, sauté onion and garlic in a pan with olive oil for about 2 minutes. Add chopped mushrooms and herbs and cook for a few minutes, until mushrooms are cooked. Drain off excess moisture, and place mixture aside in a large mixing bowl.
4. Rinse spinach and place it in a pot. Heat, covered, until spinach is wilted. Remove spinach from the pot, chop it finely, and add it to the bowl of mushrooms.

5. In the food processor, crumble the tofu. Pulse it until it forms into a ball and resembles ricotta vegan cheese; about 5-7 pulses. Add tofu and vegan mozzarella to the mixing bowl and fold everything together until mixed well.

6. Ravioli: Wet your finger and moisten all edges of 2 wonton wrap sheets. Spoon about 1 tablespoon of filling into the center of 1 wonton sheet, and cover with the another wonton sheet. Press the edges together, getting out as much air as possible. Wet the edges again and fold rim in half-inward. Press with a fork to keep edges sealed. Repeat process until all filling is used.

7. Bring a pot of water to a boil, and add the ravioli. They are done when they float to the top, about 2 to 3 minutes.

8. In the meantime, prepare pesto sauce. Heat soy milk and desired amount of pesto paste in a saucepan over low heat, just until dissolved and warm. Add ravioli and toss to coat.

9. Serve.

Penne Primavera with Alfredo Sauce

Preparation Time: 5 minutes
Cooking Time: 25 minutes
Serves: 4

Ingredients

1/4 cup olive oil + extra for sautéing
2 tablespoons wheat flour
1 cup plain nondairy milk
3 tablespoons vegan parmesan cheese
1/2 teaspoon sea salt
1/2 teaspoon black pepper
12 broccoli florets, chopped
2 carrots, julienned (cut into long thin strips)
1 red bell pepper, julienned
2-(8-ounce) boxes penne pasta, cooked according to package directions
1/2 teaspoon of crushed red pepper

Directions

1. Cook pasta according to package directions.
2. Heat a saucepan over medium heat. Add oil, then flour, and stir until it starts to slightly brown.
3. Stir in nondairy milk and vegan parmesan cheese. Stir as mixture thickens. Add salt and pepper. Remove from heat.
4. In a sauté pan, heat olive oil. Add broccoli, carrots, and bell pepper. Sauté lightly.
5. Place pasta into bowls. Pour sauce over pasta and top with sautéed vegetables.
6. Sprinkle with red pepper and parmesan.
7. Serve.

Roasted Beet Ravioli with Sage Pesto Sauce

Preparation Time: 30 minutes
Cooking Time: 1 hour
Serves: 4

Ingredients

Ravioli Filling:
5 large beets, quartered with skins on
1 package vegan wonton wrappers
5 cloves garlic, roasted
2 tablespoon chopped fresh sage
3 tablespoon vegan parmesan cheese
1/4 cup pine nuts
Olive oil, salt and pepper

Sage Pesto:
5 tablespoons chopped fresh sage
2 cups fresh parsley
1/4 cup pine nuts
3 tablespoons nutritional yeast
Fresh spinach leaves

Directions

1. In a food processor, blend all pesto ingredients, adding enough olive oil to make a smooth paste. Add salt and pepper to taste. Set aside.
2. Preheat oven to 400 degrees F.
3. Coat quartered beets in olive oil and sprinkle with salt and pepper. Wrap garlic cloves in tin foil, and place with beets in baking dish. Cook beets and garlic for 45 minutes or until beets become tender.
4. Place roasted beets, roasted garlic, sage, vegan parmesan cheese and pine nuts in food processor. Blend until smooth, adding olive oil to achieve a paste consistency.
5. Fill a won ton wrapper with a spoonful of the beet filling. Wet edges of ravioli with water and place another won ton wrapper on top. Seal edges well. Continue filling wontons until beet puree is all used.
6. Place wontons into lightly boiling salted water. Cook for only 2 to 3 minutes or until they float to the top.
7. Place a handful of spinach leaves on each serving plate, and place cooked raviolis on top of spinach.
8. Top each ravioli with a teaspoon of the pesto sauce, and a light

drizzle of olive oil and toasted pine nuts.

Roasted Red Pepper Pesto

Preparation Time: 5 minutes
Cooking Time: 20 minutes
Serves: 4

Ingredients

1-(8-ounce) packages whole-wheat pasta, dry
4 red peppers
1/2 cup unsalted walnuts
3/4 cup fresh basil
1/4 cup fresh parsley
2 or 3 garlic cloves
1/2 to 3/4 cup olive oil
Salt and pepper, to taste

Directions

1. Preheat grill or broiler and add red peppers. When skin turns black, flip them over. When both sides are mostly black, remove them from the oven and place them in a plastic bag for about 5 to 10 minutes (the steam will loosen the skin).
2. Meanwhile, boil water and begin to cook the pasta.
3. When pepper skin has loosened, peel them. Then, cut open the peppers and remove the seeds.
4. When pasta is done, drain it and return it to the pot.
5. In a food processor or blender, add walnuts, basil, parsley, garlic, and peppers. Blend well, and add pesto to noodles, toss well.
6. Add salt and pepper to taste.
7. Serve immediately.

Seared Shitakes, Walnut, and Spinach Linguine in a Butter Cream Sauce

Preparation Time: 5 minutes
Cooking Time: 15 minutes
Serves: 4

Ingredients

1 teaspoon vegan butter
12 shitake mushrooms
2 teaspoons olive oil
4 cloves garlic, minced
4-1/2 tablespoons vegan butter
2-4 cups fresh spinach
1/4 cup walnuts
1/2 cup nondairy milk
1 pound linguine pasta
Salt and pepper, to taste

Directions

1. Boil water and cook pasta according to package directions. Get out two pans: one for searing the mushrooms and one for other veggies and sauce. The pan doesn't have to be deep--a normal frying pan will do.
2. In a frying pan, add dab of vegan butter, and sear the mushrooms on medium-high heat until crispy but not burnt.
3. In a separate frying pan, heat olive oil over medium heat, and add the garlic, seared shitakes, walnuts, spinach, and vegan butter.
4. Slowly add milk and continue cooking for about 3 minutes.
5. Increase the heat to high, and boil for 1 minute. Add the vegetables and sauce to the cooked pasta. Season, to taste.
6. Serve.

Southwestern Linguine Toss

Preparation Time: 15 minutes
Cooking Time: 10 minutes
Serves: 6

Ingredients

1 pound linguine, cooked and drained
1 tablespoon olive oil
2 cups green pepper, diced
2 cups onion, diced
2 Poblano or green chili peppers, diced
3 cloves garlic, minced
1 tablespoon chili powder
1 teaspoon dried oregano
1 - 15 ounce can black beans
1 cup canned corn
2 cups ripe tomatoes, chopped
1/4 cup cilantro, chopped
Juice of one lime

Directions

1. Prepare linguine according to package instructions.
2. In a large skillet, over medium-high heat, sauté green pepper and onion in olive oil for 2 to 3 minutes until softened. Add peppers, garlic, chili powder, and oregano. Stir and sauté for an additional 2 to 3 minutes. Add black beans and corn, stir until heated.
3. Remove skillet from heat, season with salt and pepper and toss with cooked linguine.
4. Add tomatoes and cilantro, toss again.
5. Squeeze the lime juice over the finished dish.
6. Serve.

Soy Sausage and Broccoli Baked Ziti

Preparation Time: 15 minutes
Cooking Time: 50 minutes
Serves: 5 to 6

Ingredients

1-(16 ounce) box ziti
2 heads broccoli, chopped
1 (20 ounce) jar tomato pasta sauce (of choice)
1-(14 ounce) tube vegan sausage
8 ounces vegan mozzarella-style vegan cheese, shredded

Directions

1. Preheat oven to 350 degrees F.
2. Cook ziti according to directions on package and drain.
3. Meanwhile, steam broccoli until desired softness.
4. Combine ziti with pasta sauce, broccoli, and sausage balls in large rectangular dish. Top with vegan cheese.
5. Place in the oven, and bake for about 20 to 30 minutes, or until thoroughly heated and the cheese is melted.

Spinach and Mushroom Fettuccine Alfredo

Preparation Time: 30 minutes
Cooking Time: 30 minutes
Serves: 4

Ingredients

10 ounces dried porcini mushrooms
10 ounces dried chanterelle mushrooms
1-1/2 cups nondairy milk
1/2 pound fettuccine
7 ounces silken tofu
1/4 cup nutritional yeast flakes
1/8 cup vegan parmesan
3 tablespoons vegan butter
Salt and pepper, to taste
2 cloves garlic, minced
1 cup spinach, chopped
1/4 cup basil, chopped
1/4 cup parsley, chopped

Directions

1. In a bowl, soak the mushrooms in milk for 30 minutes. Strain the mushrooms and reserve the milk. Slice the mushrooms thinly.
2. Cook the pasta according to package directions, until slightly underdone, and drain. Reserve 1/2 cup pasta water.
3. In a food processor, blend the tofu, reserved milk, nutritional yeast flakes, and vegan parmesan.
4. In a medium pan on medium heat, melt vegan butter with salt. Sauté mushrooms and garlic until tender. Add the spinach and basil to the pan until they are wilted.
5. Add the tofu mixture, parsley, and pasta water to the pan. Cook low until it starts to thicken. Toss with fettuccine noodles.
6. Serve.

Tofu Florentine with Angel Hair Pasta

Preparation Time: 20 minutes
Cooking Time: 20 minutes
Serves: 4

Ingredients

2 teaspoons dried oregano, divided
2 teaspoons dried parsley, divided
2 teaspoons salt and pepper, divided
1/2 teaspoon dried basil
3 tablespoons nutritional yeast
6 cloves garlic, 3 minced and 3 peeled
1 lemon, zested
1-(14 ounce) package firm tofu
1/4 cup vegan butter (I use Earth Balance Buttery Spread)
1 cup vegetable stock
1-(14-1/2 ounce) box angel hair pasta
2 tablespoons olive oil
1-(14 ounce) package extra firm tofu, frozen overnight and then thawed in refrigerator, cut into 1-inch cubes
1 red onion, chopped
1-(12 ounce) bag frozen chopped spinach, thawed
1-(14-1/2 ounce) can petite diced tomatoes, drained

Directions

1. Heat a large pot of salted water on heat on high.
2. Pull a large skillet out for the vegetables and tofu, and get the blender ready.
3. In a blender, add 1 teaspoon oregano, 1 teaspoon parsley, 1/2 teaspoon salt, 1/2 teaspoon pepper, and all of the basil and nutritional yeast. Add 3 peeled garlic cloves, juice from 1/2 the lemon, firm tofu, vegan butter, and vegetable stock into the blender. Blend until it smooth and creamy. Set aside.
4. When the water begins to boil, add the angel hair pasta and cook according to package directions.
5. Meanwhile, heat olive oil in a large skillet over medium-high heat. Add the squeezed tofu and stir so that it soaks up the oil evenly. Cook tofu for about 5 minutes, until it starts turning a light golden color. Add remaining seasonings and lemon zest while tofu is cooking. After

stirring in seasonings, add chopped red onion and minced garlic. When the onions become tender, add the spinach. Cook until thoroughly heated. Squeeze the juice from the other half of the lemon into the pan.
6. When pasta is cooked, drain it and add it back to its cooking pot. Then, add the sauce to the pot and stir.
7. Plate the pasta first and cover it with a scoop of the tofu and spinach mixture. Top with diced tomatoes.
8. Serve.

Tofu Manicotti

Preparation Time: 1 hour
Cooking Time: 1 hour 30 minutes
Serves: 6

Ingredients

2 tablespoons olive oil
1 medium onion, chopped
6 cloves garlic, finely chopped
12 ounces vegan ground "beef"
1-(10-ounce) package frozen chopped spinach, thawed and drained
16 ounces vegan cream cheese
1-(8 ounce) package manicotti shells
3 cups spaghetti sauce (of choice)
2 tablespoons vegan margarine
2 tablespoons vegan chicken broth powder
2 tablespoons all-purpose flour
2 cups non-dairy milk
1/4 cup chopped fresh parsley
1/2 cup of vegan "parmesan" cheese
Salt and pepper, to taste

Directions

1. Preheat oven to 350 degrees F.
2. In a large skillet, heat olive oil. Add onion and sauté until they begin to turn translucent. Add garlic and sauté for one minute. Add the vegan ground beef and cook it for about 2 minutes. Add the spinach; cook it until it wilts. Stir in vegan cream cheese. Remove the skillet from the heat, and set aside.
3. In a large pot, bring water to a boil, add a little salt and cook the manicotti shells for half the time specified by their package, around 4 to 5 minutes.
4. Stuff the manicotti shells: Spoon vegan cream cheese and spinach filling into the shells, until they are full.
5. Coat a 9x13-inch baking pan with spaghetti sauce; spread sauce evenly.
6. Place stuffed manicotti shells into the prepared baking tray.
7. In a small saucepan, melt the vegan margarine. Whisk in vegan broth powder, and flour. When it begins to bubble, add the non-dairy

milk. Remove from heat and stir in parsley. Pour over the manicotti in baking tray.

8. Pour spaghetti sauce over the manicotti.
9. Cover and bake for 40 minutes.
10. Top with vegan Parmesan cheese, and place it back in the oven, baking for an additional 10 to 15 minutes, or until golden brown.

Tomato, Basil, and Roasted Pine Nut Penne

Preparation Time: 15 minutes
Cooking Time: 10 minutes
Serves: 6 to 8

Ingredients

16 ounces penne pasta
2 1/2 cups grape or cherry tomatoes, halved
1/2 cup Kalamata olives, pitted and chopped
5 large cloves garlic, pressed or minced
1/4 cup extra virgin olive oil
2 tablespoons fresh lemon juice
1 tablespoon balsamic vinegar
2 teaspoons sea salt
1/4 cup pine nuts
1/2 cup fresh basil, chopped
Freshly ground black pepper, to taste

Directions

1. Cook the pasta according to the directions on the package.
2. Meanwhile, place tomatoes in a large bowl. Add the chopped Kalamata olives, garlic, oil, lemon juice, balsamic vinegar, salt, and pepper to the giant bowl. Gently toss well to combine.
3. In a pan over medium heat, toast the pine nuts until they are aromatic and lightly browned. Stir them up occasionally to ensure that they cook evenly. This will take around 5 minutes. When they are done, remove them from the heat and set them aside.
4. When the pasta is al dente, drain it well in a colander or strainer. Add the pasta to the mixing bowl and toss it with the sauce. Mix well to combine. Add pine nuts and basil.
5. Toss lightly and serve immediately.

Tomato and Basil Spaghetti

Preparation Time: 10 minutes
Cooking Time: 20 minutes
Serves: 4 to 6

Ingredients

1 pound whole-wheat spaghetti
4 tablespoons olive oil
1 pint cherry tomatoes, halved
2 cloves garlic, minced
Salt and pepper, to taste
Basil, to taste

Directions

1. Cook whole-wheat spaghetti according to package directions.
2. Heat the olive oil in a skillet over medium heat. While skillet heats, add tomatoes and garlic. Season with salt and pepper.
3. Sauté the mixture until tomatoes are blistered and garlic is fragrant.
4. Drain pasta, reserving 1/2 cup cooking water.
5. Return pasta to pot and add the tomato mixture.
6. Add basil, toss, and serve.

Vegetable Linguine

Preparation Time: 10 minutes
Cooking Time: 20 minutes
Serves: 2

Ingredients

1/3 pound linguine
8 to 10 crimini mushrooms, sliced
1 zucchini, sliced
1 head of broccoli florets
5.75 ounces (about 1 can) black olives, pitted
3 tablespoons olive oil
Garlic and herb seasoning, to taste
Oregano, to taste
Black pepper, to taste

Directions

1. Bring water to a boil, add pasta, cover, and reduce to medium-low heat. Stir occasionally.
2. In a pan, heat 1 tablespoon of olive oil over medium heat. Add broccoli. Then add zucchini, mushrooms and olives. Stir and sprinkle with black pepper.
3. When pasta is finished cooking, drain and return to the pot.
4. When zucchini becomes soft and mushrooms start to brown, add them to the pasta and stir.
5. Add 2 tablespoons of olive oil, garlic and herb seasoning, and oregano to taste, and stir.
6. Serve.

Table of Contents

Angel Hair Pasta with Savory Mushroom Sauce
Artichoke and Angel Hair Pasta
Avocado Pasta
Basil Garlic Linguine
Creamy Macaroni & "Cheese"
Creamy Red Pepper Lentil Lasagna
Creamy Spinach Pesto
Delicious Vegan Lasagna
Easy Artichoke Pesto Pasta
Easy Cheesy Lasagna
Eggplant, Tomato, and Garlic Pasta
Eggplant Penne
Fettuccini with Chanterelle and Olive Sauce
Lentil Spaghetti
Linguine with Tomatoes
Mushroom Spinach Ravioli with Pesto Cream
Penne Primavera with Alfredo Sauce
Roasted Beet Ravioli with Sage Pesto Sauce
Roasted Red Pepper Pesto
Seared Shitakes, Walnut, and Spinach Linguine in a Butter Cream Sauce
Southwestern Linguine Toss
Soy Sausage and Broccoli Baked Ziti
Spinach and Mushroom Fettuccine Alfredo
Tofu Florentine with Angel Hair Pasta
Tofu Manicotti
Tomato, Basil, and Roasted Pine Nut Penne
Tomato and Basil Spaghetti
Vegetable Linguine

Printed in Great Britain
by Amazon